TRUE WAR STORIES™

For the fine, upstanding members of D 312th MI BN... and the rest of them, too.
— *Khai*

For my father, who served on the USS Mahogany patrolling the choppy waters of the Potomac, and who loved a good story.
— *Alex*

Eastern Afghanistan, 2013.

It felt like nothing had changed since 2011.

THE ART OF MOTORPOOL SECURITY

Two years is a drop in a bucket to the Afghans' long memories.

TYSON WALSH   PAUL WILLIAMS   MATT SOFFE

The soldiers of 2-4 IN, 4/10 MTN out of Fort Polk, LA had an advisory role. That meant maintaining a security plan, building local relationships...

...and, perhaps most importantly, looking out for one another.

Moving from FOB Tagab to Bagram Airfield (BAF) was probably our Regional East Command's *least* appreciated call.

But we got a report of a *semi-truck VBIED.**

*VBIED=Vehicle Borne Improvised Explosive Device, aka a truck bomb.

Such a monstrous VBIED, imaginary or real, could cause enough *fear* in a region to close entire camps.

The intel was assumed good, so we packed up our corner of FOB Tagab and moved to BAF.

The lovely garrison quartered us permanently in the "temporary portion" of Bagram known as *Camp Warrior*.

It was a *mess*.

Dilapidated, spread out, no visible internal security.

AFGHAN CLOTHES

Everywhere you looked were signs of *complacency*, the number-one killer of friendly forces during war.

The more seasoned soldiers felt increasingly anxious with each passing day.

We struggled to balance the main advisory mission with trying to organize some kind of *security* and *accountability*...

...at least in *our* area.

With so much going on, I latched onto one *troubling* pattern:

...And we're still getting *reports* of *break-ins*.

The *motorpool* again?

Yep. Looks like they're hitting areas with *vehicles* and *maintenance equipment*.

Maybe it's one of the *adjacent units* looking for *spare parts*.

Doubt it. Most likely it's--

"--the local Afghans."

New Mexico Military Institute, 2000.

The first time you think about fighting, it's because someone **bullies** you.

Maybe you **hit back** this time.

Maybe you **don't**.

But you promise yourself you'll **never** become like him.

After a month, I had a **routine** at Camp Warrior.

Work late, then hit the **gym** in the wee hours with a friend.

But on November 30th, my routine went to **hell**.

Hey, I'm gonna *lift*. Come keep me *honest*.

You still doing a *self-diag** after?

Yeah, you in?

Cut me some *slack* today? It's been a *long* one.

Your loss, man. Next time.

*self-diag=doing the fitness test on your own to check your progress.

US Merchant Marine Academy, 2007.

Later, fighting, even in training, becomes a way to *quiet* your mind.

You learn to stay *calm* when everything's going to hell.

You learn that even *overwhelming* advantages can still *fail*.

krak

Going somewhere?

ANP* has a *date* with the *Afghan Police* for a few days.

When's your *flight?*

*ANP=Police Advising Team, works Afghan National Police.

≡sigh≡ We need the *trucks*, so we're *driving*. We're on our way out *now*.

Bummer.* Good luck, and Godspeed.

ARMY

*Flying is much safer than driving in the 'Star

With no *battle buddy* to testify and no *Instagram* for bragging, the gym was *dull*.

The five-mile run I had planned was actually a *relief*.

Fort Benning, 2008.

I need *volunteers* for *All-Army Combatives*. Who's it gonna be?

You get a *reputation*, and you learn something *else*:

You learn some fights you *can't* win.

WHAM

Some you just have to *endure*.

HUF HUF

I couldn't stop thinking about the ANP guys.

They must have left already.

The motorpool would be almost *empty*.

4 a.m. was *prime time* for looters.

On a *hunch*, I changed my route to run past the motorpool.

Fort Carson, 2010.

You don't go **looking** for trouble.

Save--

But you won't **hesitate** when it **finds** you.

--my--

--dog!

Uh...

You learn not everyone is like that.

*Hercules, the spaniel, made a full recovery.

--!

He was a young guy, Pashtun, probably a *day laborer*.

Tons of them around.

During the *day*, that is.

No reason he should be here at *this* hour.

Besides...

Young men in Afghanistan wear *tennis shoes* for one reason alone:

They're planning to cover some *serious* ground.

Getting *security* would take an *hour*.

If I raised the alarm over some *punk kid looter,* I'd be the *laughing-stock* of the BAF.

But I couldn't *do nothing.*

I've *never* been able to do nothing.

CHK

Wadarega! Astada sho!*

ARMY

*"Stop!" in Pashto and Dari.

But this was *no* punk looter.

wham

Blasting caps, wire tools, cell phones...

...those were *IED**components.

*IED=improvised explosive device.

Enraged, terrified, but mostly determined, my mind *raced*.

The guy had enough *blasting caps* to arm an *IED factory*.

Was he holding a *trigger device?*

Would I even *feel* a *suicide vest* against my legs?

With *no backup*, I had few options.

I had to *eliminate* him *as* a threat.

So I did.

Unless there was someone nearby willing to perform a *tracheotomy* at *four in the morning*, he wasn't *coming back* from that.

That's when I saw him.

The guy I *should* have been worried about.

tonk

PAF
PAF

≥nnh≤

My *eye pro* saved my life.

Instead of the head-caving direct hit I *should* have gotten--

--AH!

--it deflected the blow *just enough* to make a difference.

My right eye was *dark*, but I could see enough to know both men were *gone*.

Every fight I've ever been in has ended the *same* way.

I *got* up.

You always have to get up, after, or you've *lost*.

nok nok

Please be the right door, *please* be the right door...

Are your eyes *green* or *brown*, Captain?

This is the *last thing* I remember from this part.

I still have *no idea* what he meant.

When the *ambulance* took off, I went *flying* out the back because I hadn't been *secured* properly.

I have *no memory* of it happening.

He's having *another* one. Watch that *needle*--

Later, they told me I'd had *seven seizures*...

...and a *Glasgow Coma Scale* of 8 before I finally *woke up* in the BAF hospital.

...just get him *stabilized* enough for *medevac*...

When you're hurt or killed in battle, they send someone out to tell your family *in person*.

I opened my eyes *moments* before they *knocked* on my wife's door.

The Keppra used to stabilize me made me *loopy*.

I took to *flashing* my chain of command and practicing my *stand-up*.

Wanna hear a *joke?*

I'm gonna *see* one if we don't keep you *covered up*.

Once I was somewhat stabilized, they medevac'd me to *Landstuhl, Germany* for treatment.

U.S. AIR FORCE

Despite my *protests*, I was sent back to the US to *recover*.

Get well soon

I spent over two months in *San Antonio* at the *Wounded Warrior Battalion* (SAMMC TBI recovery).

It would be over *a year* until the military's official investigation revealed how close we'd *really* come to *absolute disaster* that first morning in December.

The men belonged to the *Haqqani Taliban Network (HQN)*.

Their team had spent *eighteen months* hiding *remote-detonated IEDs* all over BAF.

More than *three dozen* IEDs were found, mostly in *motorpools*.

klik

HQN planned to blow all three dozen at once, then *flood* BAF with *hundreds* of *fighters*.

It could have been a *massacre*.

Instead, my attacker *flipped* on his leaders and we *derailed* the *whole attack*.

It was a nice little ending to the *bloody affair*.

But if *anything*, big or small, had happened *differently* that December morning...

...the *outcome* would have been different for us *all*.

My Vietnam Blast

ROBERT KENT   DAVE ACOSTA   ALADDIN COLLAR

Cam Ranh Bay Air Base, Vietnam. 1971.

SPLAT

DONK

drip

MILK

Son of a...

That's me, *Air Force Sergeant Robert Kent*. 22 years old.

HA HA HA HA

Shoulda *seen* your faces!

My time at Cam Ranh has run together over 50 years, but *some* things have *stayed* with me.

Asshole.

...Nice pitch.

You *know* it.

Messing with *incoming convoys*, for one.

Loved to do that.

I was *perimeter security*, mostly working *nights*.

There were six people on my patrol, spread out on different *guard towers*.

We worked with the *canine units*, too.

I'd go back and forth *checking in* on them.

*Grant?**

Still *alive* in there?

*Names changed, half for privacy and half because it was 50+ years ago.

We were across from the **POL**, aka the *Fuel Point*.

Four 2.5-million gallon containers full of *JP4*.

WARNING! FLAMMABLE

AUTHORIZED PERSONNEL ONLY

FUEL POINT
WARNING!
FLAMMABLE

The *ordnance people* warned us about what would *happen* if those babies ever *went up:*

First, everybody in a *three-mile radius* would be *incinerated.*

Then, everybody within *five miles* would die of *suffocation* from air being *sucked* into the *fire.*

In other words, it could wipe out *all* of us.

It's the kind of thing that *sticks with* you.

The Fuel Point was even *more* dangerous than the Ammo Dump...

MUNITIONS
DINING HALL
FUEL POINT

...And we had big, *big* bombs over there.

10,000- and 15,000-pounders, plus ones we called *Daisy Mays** that would clear out enough jungle to allow *8 helos* to land.

The thought of *either* of those places going up was enough to keep a guy *awake*.

Except... listen, I can neither *confirm* nor *deny* why...

ka Daisy Cutters, which could refer to a few different bombs that did the same thing.

...but let's just say I slept *good* and I *always* had an appetite.

April 25th, 1971 started like every *other* day for me.

Which is to say, it started the *night before*.

I'd been on shift since *after dinner* and still had a few hours to go.

Looks like *Sou Chin's** taking fire.

*The Korean base across the b

KABOOM

INCOMING!

--!

*Whiskey Two was my team. Oscar meant "outpost."

Let's go, *let's go!*

We would have to do that a couple more times, if you can believe it.

There were a *lot* of bombs in that dump.

We got there as fast as we could.

But it wasn't fast enough.

Hey! In here!

Grant?!

How's it **going** out there?

Can we get a **ride?**

The **fun** was **over** before we got there.

Security took out our Viet Cong **guest** while he was still **recovering** from the blast.

We sent **Grant** and **Maverick** off to be patched up, and **took over** for the rest of the night.

I **got** him. He's **my** dog.

You three walk the perimeter.

Miller, you're with me in the **Jeep.**

Maverick lost his **hearing,** but it got him sent home.

He was out of it. **Safe.**

In the end, the Viet Cong did *not* get the fuel storage area...

...but they did a number on the *Ammo Dump.*

There was *nothing* left out there.

Flat land with no trees, no telephone poles.

Phones that were in the revetment actually *melted* from the heat.

Apparently, rounds were cooking off until almost *lunchtime*.

I didn't hear for myself.

I was off shift...

...And I slept *good*.

CPL SUNSETTE WINDSLER
AND BELLA

BELLA

--War is **BIG**.

I enlisted when I was *eighteen*. Spent two years learning *Arabic.*

My 21st birthday fell on the way into *Iraq.*

I didn't have a lot of what you'd call "*real world experience.*"

Real talk? I knew precisely *dick.*

Here we go.

Home *sweet* home.

Most of this is *rubble.*

But we get the *top two floors* to ourselves.

Whoa.

YOU ARE HERE

Suddenly, though, people expected me to have *answers*.

Peace out, B-dad!

We're sure as hell *glad* to see you guys!

Our *flight out* is in a week. You catch on *fast*, right?

Listen, we got a mission tomorrow and we need to know if it's gonna be *safe* over on Haifa or--

--more pressingly, this list of cover terms seems *outdated*, can you take a look--

--and we can roll this *bad boy* up as soon as you *find* him, we're all--

--just waiting on *you guys* really, we're good to go *whenever*.

Arabic is heavily dialect-based. The learning curve was *brutal*.

Either he lost his *dog*, or he's super *into* you, sir.

I *barely* understood the locals at first.

Everyone had small things they obsessed over: little *rituals*, or *games*, or favorite *snacks*.

SQUEAK

...

As long as *that thing* was okay, the rest of it was semi-tolerable.

slap slap

Mother fu--

SQUEAK

My platoon shared one major obsession:

white chocolate macadamia cookies

Problem was, we weren't the *only ones* who loved them.

SMAK

I know the war stories people expect to hear. But *this* is the one I want to tell.

Hey!

This is a mermite. We pretend the food is better than MREs.

There was a huge *rat* in the pantry!

Look!

It got into the *macadamia!*

I *told* you that was a *thing*, K-bar.

Last week.

Yeah, but I kinda assumed you *made that up* to cover for *Reitz.*

One time!

D.Lo was an amazing platoon sergeant.

He managed to get more *macadamia goodness* a week later.

Day shift got some.

But when Nights woke up...

What the--

Get away!

...the rats had found our *new stash*.

skritch

No matter how *well* we *wrapped* the cookies...

RRRIP

...the rats ate the macadamia first *every time*.

munch

It happened *again* and *again*.

They barely *touched* anything else.

chomp rustle
snarfle

Like they *knew* how much we loved the macadamia.

Fuck you, American dogs!

X PPPT

Vive la Ratvolution!

It began to feel *personal*.

It's *cool*. I gotta get on *shift*.

I'm with Rup.

WHOMP

Still need a *driver*.

I'll grab my gear.

So a *little birdie* told me they have *macadamia* back in stock.

What's the *point?*

The *rats* will just *eat* them again.

DFAC = dining facility, where the food comes from.

--We caught our first Rebel Agent.

That's how you do it!

It was a *good* day.

This is one *ugly* dude.

Woo!

I'm not gonna lie...

skritch skritch

LIVE FREE OR DIE
LiberAte MACADAMiA!

...We got a little *weird* about it.

It wasn't until the next day that we realized our mistake.

--!

Hey, what's this *rat* still doing here?

It's in a *cage*.

Where *else* would it go?

You *know* what I mean.

Why isn't it, you know, *dead?*

See, we were *soldiers*.

Umm...

We were (theoretically) trained to kill.

People. We knew how to kill *people.*

Please, I have *42 children* and a wife!

Tiny defenseless animals were a *different* story.

Yeah, *uh...* I'm gonna get *D.Lo.*

Everyone had an idea for how to deal with the Rebel.

Poison.

We could *shoot* it.

Hit it with a *board!*

Maybe *drive it* somewhere *else?*

In the end, we decided to dunk the whole trap in a bucket of water.

Mercy, please!

We thought it would be more *humane.*

Someone, I don't remember who, brought up a story a story the previous unit told us.

They caught rats dead, with spring traps...

...Strapped them into *toy parachutes*...

...And threw them off the roof.

Afterwards they'd pin Airborne wings to the corpses before burying them.

Rest in *peace*, soldier.

Maybe we were weird, but *those* guys were weirder.

"Walking the Plank" became our go-to Rebel execution method.

The Rebels jumped on their own every time.

It felt like we were giving them a choice.

We stopped losing cookies.

Everyone started to relax.

That's when *he* showed up.

⧽Yeesh!⧼

You guys, this *rat* is *freaking* me out.

What do you *mean?*

He didn't eat the *bait*, and he's just... *...waiting.*

I swear he's *watching* me.

He's the *seventh* one, right?

Agent 007.

Maybe he thinks you're a *Bond villain.* Do a *monologue.*

I'm *telling* you, it's *weird.*

If it bugs you *that* much, I'll ask D.Lo if we can *move up* the *execution.*

We'd done this half a dozen times already.

≑sigh≑

Maybe it's a trick of memory, but *that* time felt *different*.

Agent 007 didn't panic at being carried.

He was still *waiting*.

Why couldn't we wait until *after* dinner?

≑snerk≑

Because it's *scaring* K-Bar.

Shut *up!* *Dude*, that thing is *creepy*.

It's probably *sick*.

Okay, *little guy*, let's put you out of your *misery*.

There was a long moment where we thought we'd have to *shake* him out.

Just like the others, though, Agent 007 jumped.

There he goes!

That's when things went *sideways*.

As soon as he cleared the ledge, 007 threw his legs out wide.

It was like he *knew* how to slow his fall.

...Are you guys *seeing* this?

Then, right before he hit the ground, Agent 007 tucked his shoulder--

--and *rolled*, like he was doing a PLF*.

*PLF = Parachute Landing Fall. How airborne troopers land.

Is he--

He's getting up. He's *alive!*

Is this actually *happening?!*

It was a rough year, but at last our relief arrived.

We're *sure* as *hell* glad to see you guys!

You catch on *fast*, right?

We told the newbies about the Rebels, but I don't think they believed us.

...So then he gets up and *walks away!*

150 feet down and he just shook it off.

If I hadn't seen it, I wouldn't have believed us, either.

Did everybody *go potty?*

It didn't matter, though. We were done. We made it.

Okay, let's *roll out.*

We were going home.

∋Pfft!∈ American dogs.

REBELS OF MACADAMI

KHAI KRUMBHA

JEFF MCCOMSE

DEE CUNNIFF

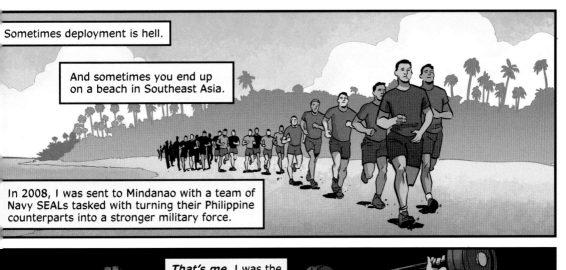

Sometimes deployment is hell.

And sometimes you end up on a beach in Southeast Asia.

In 2008, I was sent to Mindanao with a team of Navy SEALs tasked with turning their Philippine counterparts into a stronger military force.

That's me. I was the token Air Force guy.

Don't get me wrong. It was *hard work*.

It was also *great company*, and all the *lumpia* we could eat.

Little did we know our beach deployment would turn *deadly serious*.

Because in a village 20 miles from our base...

...something *terrible* was about to happen.

POK POK

Bye, mami!

I'll be *home* in an hour. Do your *homework*!

⹂uugh!⹁ I know!

vroom

TUK TUK TUK

⹂tsk⹁

VROOM

Her name was *Rosamie.*

Her family wasn't rich by our standards...

...but they were *rich enough.*

klik

The kidnappers tell the family to deliver money in *one week.*

The family calls the *local government...*

...and *guess who* the local government calls.

Within 5 hours of Rosamie being taken, our mission is changed from training to *counter kidnap for ransom.*

What's the *surprise briefing* for?

Beats me.

It's a job we can take on easily, but it changed our mentality.

Fun time's over. Someone's *life* is on the line.

DAYS UNTIL RANSOM:

Problem is, if you want to get *lost*, the Philippines is a *great* place to do it.

Jungle on one side of the beach, and on the other, *islands* so small they don't show up on maps.

The hunt was on.

While I and a colleague make phone calls and scour all available reports on the local area and police dossiers on *potential captors*...

...another part of the team asks *locals* if anyone saw what happened or recognized the captors.

We found their *vehicle*.

They must have gone *on foot* from here.

Others trace the *route* of the kidnappers.

Roger. Can you pick up *tracks?*

Yeah, I got a *trail*.

There's a *beach* about a *klick* away.

How much you wanna *bet* they were heading *there?*

The *fishermen* at the beach say they saw an *outrigger* they didn't recognize heading *south-southwest* about an *hour* after Rosamie was taken.

VAN

There's a *ton* of *tiny islands* in that direction...

Back at base, we're linking all the information together to see if we can narrow down suspects and a search radius.

Someone probably *brought* the outrigger *from* the island, which means the likely *maximum range* from the beach is however far you can get on a *half-tank of gas...*

Meanwhile, the photos and threats keep coming.

DAYS UNTIL RANSOM: 5

Which narrows it down to *here*.

Time for the *eagle* to fly

The ScanEagle is a lightweight reconnaissance UAV which records and sends a video feed.

We sent it over the islands in our search area and compared what it saw to recent satellite imagery.

We were looking for signs of *human habitation*.

Specifically, signs of *changes* in human presence.

I got one!

Except it wasn't just *one* island.

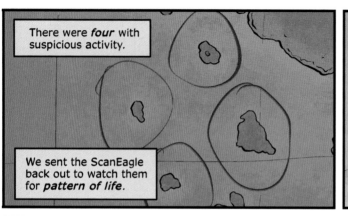

There were *four* with suspicious activity.

We sent the ScanEagle back out to watch them for *pattern of life.*

How many people on the island?

What does a normal day look like?

Who's breaking that pattern?

DAYS UNTIL RANSOM: 4

We're not getting anywhere.

So we sent in a man wearing a button camera.

I'm not going to *pass.*

Innocent people won't *care* if there's a *stranger* in their village.

Yeah, that's what I'm *afraid* of.

Only *guilty people* will.

Do I have to go in *unarmed?*

Yes.

But we'll have the *ScanEagle* on *overwatch.*

So if anything goes *wrong...*

...we'll *be there* to back you up.

Nothing struck us as *out of place* in the first two villages.

The third village just seemed... *empty*.

The fourth village--

slap
slap

slap

"Only guilty people will react."

This is the hardest part.

You want to look back.

You want to *run*.

You want to bust in there and see if that really was the victim.

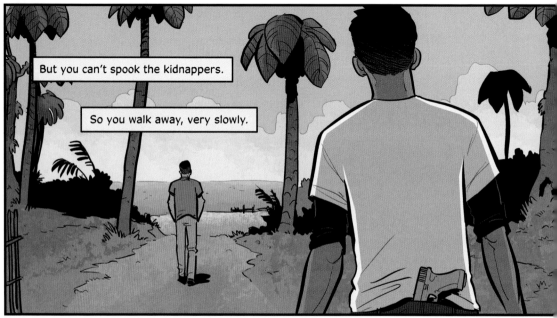

But you can't spook the kidnappers.

So you walk away, very slowly.

I think I *got* something...

DAYS UNTIL RANSOM: 3

What do you think?

This is *their* op now. And we want to set them up for success.

US troops are not allowed to conduct combat in this region. Rosamie's rescue is up to her countrymen: the *Philippine SEALS* we've been training.

For the honor of the Philippine SEALS.

And for Rosamie.

So we practice.

And we *practice.*

KRAK

One more time!

=grumble=

They're *not ready*, are they?

No, sir.

DAYS UNTIL RANSOM: 1

Do we have a *choice?*

Also negative, sir.

All right! Get to the *boats!*

--?

We got her.

Hi there, Rosamie.

It's so *good* to see you.

We're going to take you *home*, okay?

Okay.

Ready to *go*, chief?

Ready!

Our trainees saved a life today.

It doesn't get much better than that.

Mami!

Papi!

The *whole village* came out for Rosamie's return.

Oh, baby...

And us? We went back to base...

CALENDAR FROM KIDS

HAPPY 43RD BIRTHDAY CARD

POWER BARS

EAR PLUGS

PICTURES OF WIFE + KIDS

Lt. Col Barker Flash

37

DOG (BURNER)

FAMILY PHOTOS

"THAT IS ALL THAT IS ON MY LOG TODAY. IS IDF ATTACKS,"

SURVIVAL VEST

HARNESS

CHECKLIST

HELMET BAG

G-SUIT

≈sigh≈

skritch

I gotta admit, that feels *really* good.

FOB* *Lion* is *too small* to land helicopters inside the walls, so we've got a *short drive* up the road.

*FOB = Forward Operating Base.

We got *free wifi*, a *DVD library*, and 24/7 self-serve scoop *ice cream* in the DFAC.

Wow. Sounds like a business-class *hotel*. Or a *B&B.*

We're the *guests* of the *Panjshiris* here, under their *protection*.

That's why we don't wear *body armor*, and we drive *armored SUVs* instead of our *MRAPs.**

We don't want to *insult* them.

*MRAP = Mine-Resistant Ambush-Protected truck.

This isn't how I thought I'd go to Afghanistan.

In 2010, I was one of over 3,000 citizen-soldiers preparing to deploy with 2nd Brigade Combat Team, 34th Infantry "Red Bull" Division.

The brigade's one-year mission was to *clear, hold, and build...*

Clear the countryside of weapons and bad guys.

Hold the territory and make it safe for Afghan civilians.

Build up the Afghan government: Army, police, courts, even the economy.

Your tax dollars at work: Send a small town's worth of your fellow farmers, bankers, firefighters, teachers, and neighbors halfway around the world and have them help create a new nation.

Brown? *Not so fast!*

It was the largest call-up of Iowa troops since World War II, and I was part of it.

At least, I *thought* I was.

The personnel officer (S1) had, for 18 months, misinterpreted my eligibility to deploy.

Up until the last minute, the S1 swore I could still deploy. That I'd just "turn into a pumpkin" upon the unit's return.

This proved incorrect.

Instead of deploying, I got retired.

But: I had civilian press credentials.

So I bought my own body armor, used up all my wife's airline miles, and went to Afghanistan anyway.

I embedded with the Red Bull as civilian media.

Historically, Panjshir is not a welcome mat.

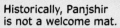

Greetings from Sunny PANJ

It is an anvil.

The word *Panjshir* means *five lions*, after an 11th-century story of five pious Muslim brothers who protected the valley.

In the early 1980s, Ahmad Shah Massoud, the Lion of Panjshir, and his fighters successfully fought off repeated attacks by Soviet troops.

From 1996 to 2001, they also kept the Taliban out of the valley.

SHIR
the Valley of Lions

SHAH MASSOUD.

Massoud is now a martyr, assassinated two days before 9/11.

THE LIONS' GATE.

His picture is plastered on walls and windows throughout the national capital of Kabul, and the surrounding provinces.

MASSOUD'S GRAVESITE.

His tomb in Panjshir, a modernist minaret surrounded by rusting husks of Soviet war machinery, has become a place of pilgrimage.

After catching up with Eipperle, I met *Bill Martin* from the US State Department. He's the director of a *PRT** for Panjshir, and the engine behind the tourism conference.

Welcome! You missed *hiking* and *sight-seeing,* but you can hear all about it at *dinner!*

*PRT = Provincial Reconstruction Team.

Our host will be *Deputy Provincial Governor* Abdul Rahman Kabiri!

Deputy? Where's the governor?

He's on *vacation.*

That seems... *ironic?*

Municipal Guest House, Bazarak District, Panjshir.

The tourism conference attendees were businesspeople from overseas and here in Afghanistan, economic development experts from the US, and a handful of media.

It was a well-traveled bunch.

How *lovely!*

Very nice.

Wouldn't mind staying *here*, rather than the *FOB...*

Still, they seemed impressed.

Eipperle will leave his armored vehicle to engage the assassin.

No!

BRAKKA BRAKKA

BLAM BLAM

He will take the gunman down.

In the exchange, he will be shot himself.

BAM

Everyone **out!**

Get out of your bunks for a count!

NOW!

Throughout the ship, sailors were going **wild** as men and women scrambled to their duty stations.

A full-scale **search and rescue operation** was launched for the missing crewman.

WHUP WHUP WHUP WHUP

All hands on deck.

All except the **Marines**, of course.

≡sigh≡

I **knew** it was too much to hope I'd gotten **rid** of one of you.

As you **were**.

US MARINES

Interviews were conducted.

Hours of security footage were reviewed.

And it was on that footage that the *truth* was revealed.

That evening, on the fantail of the ship, in anticipation of their return home...*

*also because their first sergeant found her during a health and comfort inspection.

...a group of Marines assembled to send off a beloved shipmate.

With full military honors, they consigned their *faithful companion* to the sea.

MAN OVERBOARD!

MATT MOORES   **PETER KRAUSE**   **KELLY FITZPATRIC**

ON THE BRIDGE OF
THE USS BATAAN

RADAR
OPERATOR

For centuries, the land that would become Iraq thrived as a center of learning and enlightenment, with a vibrant Jewish community tracing its roots to ancient Babylon.

In the early 20th century, one third of Baghdad's population was Jewish.

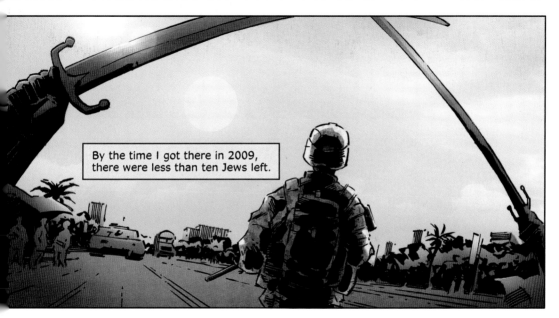

By the time I got there in 2009, there were less than ten Jews left.

There were even fewer Jews in Afghanistan.

WHUP WHUP WHUP WHU

Specifically, there was *one* Jew left in Afghanistan by 2011.

Zablon Simintov.

WHUP WHUP WH

I never actually met the guy.

KAF Community Center

I was beginning to think the Army was deliberately sending me to places that were...

...less than friendly to my people.

So imagine my surprise when I discovered that among our US and NATO allies...

...we had a pretty active Jewish community all stationed at Kandahar Airfield.

I loved going to Friday night Shabbat services.

It was something to look forward to every week.

How can I e-mail the help desk that I can't log in to the *SIPR* when the system won't *let* me log in to the *SIPR* so I can e-mail the help desk?!

Through boring days...

AWWOOOOOOOOOOOOOOO

ROCKET ATTACK

Less boring days...

ROCKET ATTACK

WHUP WHUP WHUP W

Even less boring days...

...I always knew what was waiting for me on Friday nights.

And although General Order #1 meant we couldn't have alcohol...

...we were authorized one small glass of wine for Shabbat and holiday ceremonial purposes.

Manischewitz never tasted so sweet.

Holidays away from home didn't seem quite as bad.

"A great *miracle* happened there."

We even had an actual rabbi for some stretches...

...elohanu meloch ha'olam...

...when the Jewish chaplain was in theater doing battlefield circulations.

When the rabbi wasn't there, one of us would be designated as the lay leader to oversee and coordinate the Jewish services.

Which ended up being *me*.

Which is how I got the *phone call*.

RIIIIING RII

Hello?

A Jewish soldier had been wounded in an IED attack and I was listed as the contact for Jewish services.

They needed me to come down to the CSH Role 3 for a purple heart ceremony, since the Jewish chaplain was at another FOB.

Zhari

The soldier and his buddy had been hit on a route just outside FOB Howz-E-Madad.

I had just been there a few days ago.

That could have been me.

We had just brought in new school and medical supplies for the area.

MARIO WORLD TIME

I liked going to Howz-E-Madad because I loved saying the name.

IT'S-A ME MARIO HOW'S-A MY DAD?

WELCOME TO HOWZ-E-MADAD

It didn't seem very funny now.

shuff

I couldn't help feeling guilty.

PRAYER BOOK
JEWISH PERSONNEL
ARMED FORCES
UNITED STATES

KAF Community Center

This was my third deployment.

Even my friends back home couldn't help pointing out that I was pushing my luck.

My friends could be real assholes sometimes.

Hey! Don't get blown up.

I'm gonna try *real hard* not to.

But if you *do* get blown up?

Don't die.

Okay, thanks.

Because if you get *blown up* and you *don't die* and you come *home?*

Dude. You're gonna get *so* many *chicks!*

...Now I had to figure out what to say to someone who *really did* get blown up.

I wasn't a real rabbi.

I wasn't even a chaplain's assistant.

I was just a guy who answered the phone.

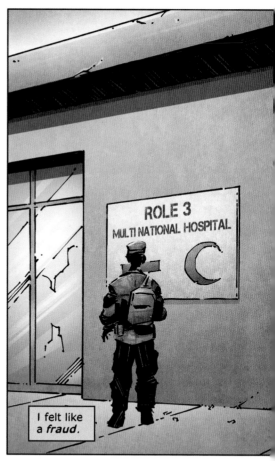

ROLE 3
MULTI NATIONAL HOSPITAL

I felt like a *fraud*.

There's a soldier *medevac'd* in from Howz-E-Madad?

He's in ICU. *That way*.

This poor guy deserved *real* spiritual counsel.

Then I remembered something our rabbi said:

The *traditions*, the *prayers*, they're just there to *guide* us, to provide a framework.

It doesn't *always* have to be a *specific* prayer or specific words.

It's whatever helps us hear *what* we need to hear, *when* we need to hear it. *That's all*.

I was immediately struck by how much like a real hospital it looked.

I don't know what I expected.

I need 15cc of *morphine* and an *extra olive*, stat!

I found my guy.

He wasn't a regular at our Shabbat dinners.

He was pretty banged up and had taken shrapnel to the face.

But he was in one piece.

Not all his buddies were so lucky.

The general pinned his medal on him and I read a traditional prayer for healing.

Mi Shebeirach avoteinu v'imoteinu...

And then we were alone.

≡whew≡

Can I...?

Huh?

Oh!

Sure.

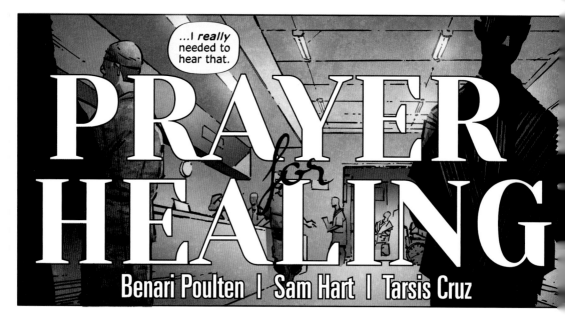

PRAYER for HEALING

Benari Poulten | Sam Hart | Tarsis Cruz

GAS
GEAR

Camp Lejeune, North Carolina.

Feb 29, 2004. 0200 hours.

BAM BAM BAM

Wake up!

This is *not* a drill!

I had been on *Barracks Duty* since 0800.

My unit was on the *highest level* of air alert, ready to *deploy* at any moment.

Thirty minutes ago--

This is the *real deal*.

Got *the call* from Division:

You're activated.

0205 hours: Battalion Duty Hut

I can't say *where* we're going...

1000 hours: Battalion Common Area

...But I love you, Dad.

VROOM

CAMP LE
HOME
EXPEDITIO
FORCES IN R

Tell everyone I'll be *okay*.

1400 hours: Flight Line, Marine Corps Air Station Cherry Point.

As the Senior Marine from my Scout Sniper Team, I was responsible for getting everyone there until the rest of the platoon arrived.

We're gonna be the *first* on the ground--

Tip of the spear!

--so I'm gonna *need* your *SSN*, *blood type*, next of *kin*...

...And all your *serialized gear*, too.

GROOOAN

1800 hours.

I've been awake over 30 hours now without any real rest.

This is why we train so hard. Moments like these.

I dunno, man.

Six mags doesn't *feel* like enough *ammo.*

The unpredictability. Hurry up and wait...

If we need more than *180 rounds*...

...we're *already* fucked.

Roger, Snake Bite, this is INDIA-SIX-ACTUAL.

It's the Company Commander, Captain ███████.

Are there **Marines** in the area? Over.

I know their patrol routes. No one is out there.

Negative, over.

584

He reloads, unaware that we have him.

Is he shooting at **us?**

592

His wrist bounces after every recoil. He's reckless; untrained.

BANG BANG

Shooting this direction. A pistol isn't effective at this range.

We're not his targets. I scan and check for wounded in the area.

Negative, over.

There's a **second** shooter.

And just like that, it's over.

At our debrief, the captain explained he was following our rules of engagement.

What the 💀⊘⚡#, yo?!

Shit *always* happens when *you're* on post!

It's not like we're *planning* it...

Hey! I heard y'all could have had the first *platoon kill!*

What the 💀⊘⚡# *happened?* Let's *talk*, Vaca.

The Chief Scout: our platoon's senior NCO.

Ever heard of "*better to* say *sorry* than to ask for *permission*"?

Nothing *personal*, but █████ is gonna *lead* the team now.

Set up a **48-hour OP**.

There's **banana fields** for cover--

We continued to plan missions...

Recon the **AO**.

Confirm the **target**...

...And **initiate** the **raid**.

...That were based on bad information.

What the 🐙☠️⚡#, gents?

Extract already?

There's **no** farm **or** banana fields.

I got a **bad** feeling about this...

You may be wondering how I ended up in the *Air Force* after that...

You've taken *too many* sick days.

You're *fired**.

*These two facts officially have nothing to do with each other. I was in a right-to-work state, so they can fire me without cause, which is what they're doing despite having just said they have a cause.

It's *your* fault.

Here's your *ticket.*

You missed *too many* classes.

You *fail.*

Again.

You're *late* again. You're *fired.*

I'm sorry, we just... *can't* let you *stay* any longer.

You *need* to find your *own* place.

The truth is, I didn't see what else I could do.

I would like to *sell myself* into *servitude* for *four years*, please.

Sure! It'll be *great!*

You *won't* be able to *tell* them you're *trans*.

Yeah, but they won't be able to *ask*.

It'll be *fine*.

Spoiler: It will *not* be fine.

I won't be able to *see* you for a *long time*.

The *recruiter* says I'll probably be able to get *stationed* nearby.

It won't be *that* bad.

Your *number* came up!

I've *changed* my mind.

I don't want to *do* this.

*Too late!**

*It wasn't too late. Recruiters just lie.

...ALL ENEMIES, FOR**EIGN AND DOMESTIC**...

On the plane I learned I wasn't actually the *most* unfortunate new recruit.

Hey there. I'm *Poole*.

I'm joining the *Navy*.

Wait, so your *name* is...

Seaman...

...Poole?

We got up at *4am* on the East Coast, which is 3am here, and took a *four-hour flight* to get here. So *why* are we arriving *after midnight?*

≡tsk!≡
Hurry up and *wait*.

Move!

Move!

Move!

Males on the *right*!

Females on the *left*!

Fall in!

Stand *completely* still until I *order* you to move!

This is your *last* chance!

If you're *not serious* about wanting to be here, *raise your hand!*

Uh...

I DID NOT TELL YOU TO MOVE, MAGGOT!

Well, 💀⚙️⚡#.

YOU WILL PERFORM A MINIMUM OF FIFTY SIT-UPS IN SIXTY SECONDS! BEGIN!

TIME'S UP! IF YOU DIDN'T DO FIFTY, YOU'RE A MISERABLE PIECE OF SHIT AND I HATE YOU!

27... 28...

YOU WILL RUN ONE POINT FIVE MILES! MALES WILL COMPLETE THIS RUN IN 11:57 OR LESS! FEMALES WILL COMPLETE THIS RUN IN 13:56 OR LESS!

FIFTEEN MINUTES?! YOU'RE A DISGRACE!

TIME'S UP! THOSE OF YOU WHO DID NOT MEET THE REQUIREMENTS* ARE TRULY DESPICABLE HUMAN GARBAGE!

17... 18...

Over the next four years, my ability to do these tasks was *never* required for me to do my job, only to pass more arbitrary fitness tests.

There was absolutely *no reason* to subject me to that abuse.

None.

45 pushups in 60 seconds for men; 27 for women. Women could opt to do pushups with their knees on the ground.

I survived BMT and was transferred from the hellfires of San Antonio to McChord Field, where it was always raining.

Welcome to your *new home!*

I'm *Jaws.*

I was supposed to be doing communications cable and antenna maintenance.

The stuff they taught us in tech school seemed kinda fun.

It wasn't for another few months until I realized how little the actual job had to do with the tech school.

This is *MSgt Wolf.* He's *in charge* of the shop.

You're going to need a *callsign.*

Don't worry, I *already* came up with it before I ever *met* you!

I saw you got *stupid high* test scores in training and almost *washed out* on the *physical* tests!

So your callsign is *Brain!*

HA HA

HI, I'M WINKY.

So you're *Winky and the Brain!*

Get it!?

This is gonna be *great!*

Narf!

≥sigh≤

Sorry about the *dumb* callsign.

They call me *Smoke...* because I smoke.

So I can *sympathize.*

AWW! **NICE ONE, JAWS!**

Fart jokes? **Really?**

That wasn't a fart joke!

This is a **fart joke:**

What's the **acronym** for the **Security Forces Squadron?**

It's an **initialism**, not an acronym.

SFS!

But what SFS **really** stands for is **Shit/Fart Separator.**

That's the thing that **separates** your **shit** from your **fart** so you can **fart** without **shitting.**

As you get **older**, your SFS **wears out**, so you gotta be more **careful** when you fart.

It's quite **embarrassing** when you **shart** yourself!

NICE ONE, JAWS!

HYUK HYUK

Truly, I'd found myself in a hotbed of intellectual discourse.

Just got off the **phone** with the **lieutenant.** She's **coming over.**

Somebody better go **hide** all the **porn** in the bathroom.

The what.

NOT IT!

Yep. This **really is** how we do things **around here.**

Awesome.

CARS

PORN MAGS

*It will, but not until 2019.

You're probably thinking that this isn't a deployment story.

Buddy, that's what I thought too.

But, two years into my stay at the shop...

The *commander* says we need to *send* someone for this *deployment cycle* to augment *Security Forces.*

You're *basically worthless* anyway, so I picked *you!*

Gee, *thanks.*

So I won't even be doing my *job* there?

You'll be separating the *shit* from the *farts.*

By *standing around* holding a gun you're *not allowed* to *fire.*

It's been *months*, and my wrist *still* hurts.

They *wouldn't* send someone who's *already injured?*

Sorry. *Doctor* already *cleared* you.

Never even *saw* a damn doctor...

Why not send *Winky?*

He's *never* been *deployed;* surely *he's* due.

...*Nobody* deserves to have me send them *Winky.*

2007.

Balad Air Base/Camp Anaconda, Balad, Iraq.

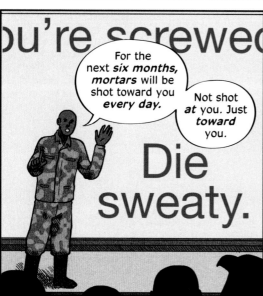

ou're screwed

For the next *six months, mortars* will be shot toward you *every day.*

Not shot *at* you. Just *toward* you.

Die sweaty.

I'm *stuck* in here with *eleven* guys?

It'll be *fine.*

=sigh=

♪ Hey there, Delilah, what's it like in New York City? It's a thousand miles away... ♪

It's actually ten thousand miles from Iraq to NYC, but hey, it's a metaphor.

My first assignment was watching over a Turkish work crew.

They *joked* that this assignment would be like *watching paint dry*.

How is there something *more monotonous* than that?!

We're watching *someone else* watch *concrete* dry.

I tried to be "*one of the guys.*"

How you say "*sunglasses*"?

Goon-ass... ...Godzooky.

Güneş gözlüğü.

Eh... *okay.* Same-same.

Okay, okay. How you say... ≠hmm≠ ...memeler?

Boobs. It's *boobs.* You...

...you *know* this.

You've been *screaming* it at every woman you've seen *all day.*

Heh heh. "*Buwbs!*"

Omigawd, *what's that?!* How you say?! *How you say?!*

Eh... *çakal,* maybe?

Jackal? **JACKAL?!**

It's a jackal?

Iraq was hot, soul-crushingly boring, lonely...

...and awash in toxic masculinity.

The highlight of my deployment was the couple of times I got to go to the Army side of the base.

They had a *Popeye's.*

I tried to fit in.

I even learned to smoke so I could hang out with the *"other guys."*

I quit a week later because smoking is boring and the *"other guys"* were boring.

I couldn't talk to any women because the guys aggressively competed for their attention.

And, worst of all, I was jealous of everyone involved in that mildly abusive social power struggle, because I had no place in it.

Whatcha bet I can make it *this* time?

The *entirety* of my *self-esteem.*

KLONK

Yess!

The once an' future *champeen!*

Six months later, I returned to McChord.

It was raining.

brr!

It's **75 degrees** out!

It's **not** cold!

That's literally **65 degrees colder** than I was **48 hours** ago.

It's **cold.**

I **finally** got to see a doctor.

Oh, **yeah**, you've got a **broken bone** here in your wrist.

I KNOW!

So, feeling any **better**, dysphoria-wise?

Are you ☠☢⚡#◪◍✳ **kidding** me?

... I'll **put that down** as a "no."

Okay.

That's it?

"Okay?!"

I'll listen to *whatever* you feel like *sharing*.

But *yeah*, it's okay.

Oh. *Okay*.

I grew up in *Hawaii* and *SoCal*, dude.

What, I was gonna say you're going to *hell*?

Maybe... *don't* call me *dude?*

Oh. It's *gender neutral* where I grew up.

But not for *you*, huh? Okay.

I *have* to get the 🕸⊙⚡# *out* of the military.

You've been *saying* that literally since *day one.*

Well, *now* you know *another* reason why.

I'm going to tell the *first sergeant.*

Or *somebody.*

That sounds *risky* as *hell*, du--

Sorry.

*Don't Ask/Don't Tell only pertained to homosexuality. It didn't say anything about trans people, because Congress st
doesn't know that we're not just The Gays. That technicality gave me the confidence to go through this little song & d

I talked about *that thing* we talked about to my *therapist* and the *JAG* and the *first sergeant.*

Oh, du--

Good news, The Brain! You've got a *new* assignment!

You're going to *Tokyo*, you *nerd!*

Nothing happened.

It's *fi--*

HA HA HA HA HA HA HA HA HA HA HA HA

I've wanted to go to Japan for years. For *nerd reasons*, as Wolf said.

It was my number-two base of preference, after home.

Huh. That would've been *nice.*

But I'm *not* going.

I'm *not re-upping* my contract.

I'd report to Tokyo...

...*Three weeks* before my *contract* is up.

I assume you'll make this *go away* and save the Air Force a pair of *international plane tickets?*

Four years later, I caught up with Hilary...

Oh, you're playing *roller derby* now?

That's a *thing?*

Yeah, it's a *thing*. Do you want to *come* to my next *bout?*

shove

barge

LAK

KLAK

KLAK

smooch

kiss

smooch

mash

Want to get *married?*

I *do!*

Ten years after I came out to Hilary, I was starting my transition.

It's really happening.

This is terrifying.

This is the office of Dr. DoesTransHealthcare. How can I help you?

I...

I'm...

Oh no.

I'm sorry.

I'll call you back.

How can I help you?

I would like to start HRT.

Great!

Here's some titty skittles!

Wow.

Wow.

Buwbs.

nstead, the whole company was
ack together, however briefly.

Eight of us, packed into the flimsy,
plywood and corrugated metal
18' by 36' B-Hut where we lived.

INCOMING   INCOMING   INCOMING   INCOMING   INCO

Hilarity can strike
in the oddest ways.

For us, it was when the
incoming alarm went off.

ING   INCOMING   INCOMING   INCOMING   INCOMI

Whereas angels heralded the arrival
of the Savior in Bethlehem, its dulcet
tones heralded the arrival of some
shoddily made 107mm rocket.

Aaand...

KABOOM

Our attitude, by this time, was less
than responsible. We just rolled out
of bed and onto the floor...

...it's *Merry Christmas* from them.

...rather than donning protective
gear and heading to a cat urine-
filled bunker, as was SOP.

On this holiest of nights, when God came to Earth in flesh incarnate to bring peace and goodwill to men, we made a compromise with the procedures:

We would not abandon the warmth of our unarmored shelter, but we would gear up, in deference to the solemnity of it all.

Helmets were placed over our bedhead with care, in the hope no Taliban rockets would visit us there.

Does Santa come to Afghanistan?

BOOM

Alarms heralded more *season's greetings* from the Taliban, winging their inaccurate way to impact somewhere on the base.

Was it worth it, to some freezing, bearded fighter, to set up his makeshift launching system and fire off a munition that was as likely to blow up in his face as it was to hit an American interloper?

Apparently.

NCOMING
NCOMING
NCOMING

Uh...

KRACKLE   KRK   KRACKLE   KKKKK

We dutifully acquiesced to common sense by adopting the prone position.

Which is where I lost it, laying on the dusty plywood floor, in a helmet, body armor, and a damned *plaid onesie*.

≡snerk≡
Heh.

The profound absurdity of my own piece of this war, all striking me, right then.

What is it?

≡hee≡
Nothing.

The height of absurdity would have been if I was snuffed out in a onesie, but that didn't happen.

HA HA HA HA
HA HA HA HA
HA HA HA
HA HA HEE

The cold-fingered fighters hightailed it before someone dropped a 500lb bomb on them.

ALL CLEAR ALL CLEAR

Ahhh, peace on Earth.

Merry Christmas, Khaareji!

by JONATHAN BRATTE
EOIN MARRO
DEE CUNNIFF

Okinawa, Spring 2002.

Airman Jennings is not a front-line fighter.

Airman Jennings is a Tech Controller.

He fixes circuits and computers.

But there aren't enough Airmen trained to secure the base...

IRMAN JENNINGS THE IMPALER

randon Davis Jennings   PJ Holden   Kelly Fitzpatrick

...And Osama Bin Laden's terrorists are *everywhere*.

Everyone is suddenly carrying those *brown sacks*.

They *gather* together.

No one is working any more!

Airman Jennings holds his breath.

Have they been *waiting* this whole time to *strike?*

Will they brandish *guns* and *knives*...

...showing Airman Jennings how they will *kill* him? Or...

rustle

...the bags are so *small*.

Will *these terrorists* employ...

A PLASTIC BAGGIE OF **ANTHRAX?**

A VIAL OF **SMALLPOX?**

AN AEROSOL CAN OF **SARIN GAS?**

ANYTHING IS POSSIBLE!

THE **ORGANIZATION** THESE CONTRACTORS WORK FOR **ORDERED** MEN TO THEIR **DEATHS**, AND THEY **WENT**.

THE **SMOKING TOWERS** PROVED THEY WEREN'T **AFRAID** TO **DIE**.

Unlike Airman Jennings.

Airman Jennings is *afraid* to *die*.

That's why he's *angry* to be armed with nothing more than this *radio* that his superiors want him to call a *brick*.

He is *not safe*, and he is *alone*.

He needs a *pla[...]*

Camp Victory, Iraq. December 2006.

The worst thing about a classified staff job, other than never leaving the base?

The monotony.

Especially when there are only two of us in the whole country that can do our specific job.

That means twelve-hour shifts, every day.

Weekends do not exist.

Holidays do not exist.

But you don't complain. Ever.

There are young soldiers out there that would kill to have this well-protected job.

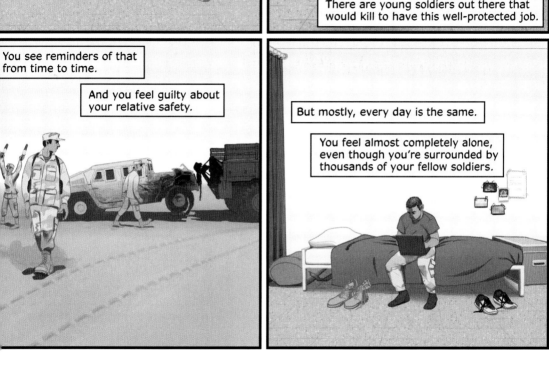

You see reminders of that from time to time.

And you feel guilty about your relative safety.

But mostly, every day is the same.

You feel almost completely alone, even though you're surrounded by thousands of your fellow soldiers.

The only really good moments are the meals spent with Technical Sergeant Craig Cannon.

We're both from the same unit back home.

Hey, Captain!

Saved you a seat!

He's my opposite, working the job for the twelve hours I'm not there.

He's also the only thing that makes this life tolerable.

You want to go look at the *set-up* afterwards?

Shit, *yeah*, of course.

Craig and I always meet for a meal when we hand the shift over to one another.

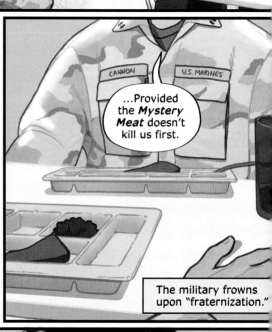

...Provided the *Mystery Meat* doesn't kill us first.

CANNON   U.S. MARINES

The military frowns upon "fraternization."

That means, as an officer, I'm supposed to maintain a working relationship with Sergeant Cannon, not a friendship.

HA HA HA HA HA HA HA HA

Well, that's damn near impossible.

Aside from the anticipation of the next day's WWE show, that day's lunch with Craig wrapped up like every other one.

See you on the other side!

I was happy to have spent time with my friend, but sad to know it would be twelve hours before we got to chat again.

Craig headed back to his trailer for some sleep, and I headed in to man the desk.

Just like every other day.

Huh?

I was unaware this was about to become my *worst* day.

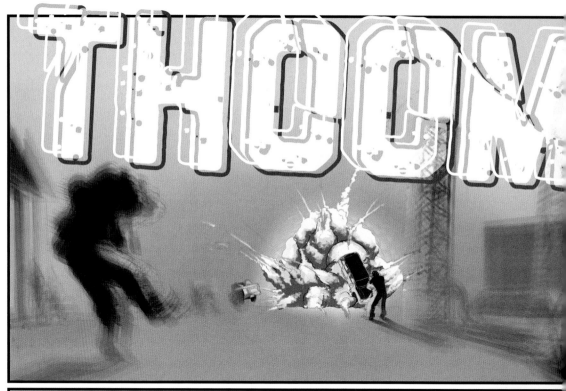

The WWE workers just stood there in shock.

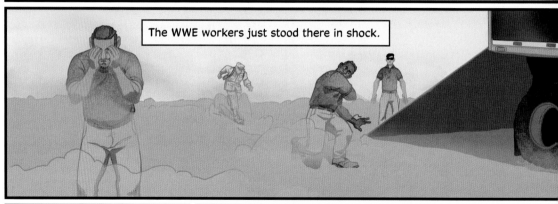

They didn't know that the first explosion is often followed by more as the enemy adjusts fire.

GET COVER!

As we waited for the *all clear*, I realized something.

Craig had been headed in that direction.

I don't think I've ever sprinted so fast in my life as I did after the all clear sounded.

Colonel Wingfield!

HUF HUF

Have you seen *Sergeant Cannon?*

No.

Not since he *clocked off* shift before lunch.

Without hesitation, the colonel gave me permission to leave my post.

To see if Craig had made it to his trailer.

I was two times lucky.

I was sent to Thailand and not Vietnam...

...and I was selected for the Military Police.

I had no desire to be a policeman, but it kept me out of the Infantry.

Not that being an MP was without dangers.

MP duties included patrolling the base...

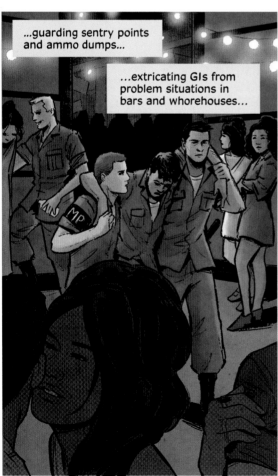

...guarding sentry points and ammo dumps...

...extricating GIs from problem situations in bars and whorehouses...

...and providing jeep escorts for bomb convoys.

Bombs arrived by ship to Sattahip, on the coast of Thailand, every single day.

It's hard to describe the number of bombs I saw.

Tens of thousands of bombs.

Acres of bombs.

They were offloaded 24 hours a day, seven days a week, to trucks that were dispatched to either ammo dumps or air bases up-country:

U-Tapao, Korat, Udorn, Ubon, Takhli, Nakhon Phanom.

The majority of the air strikes that hit North Vietnam in these years originated from bases in Thailand.

Bombs were moved from the coast to the air bases on truck convoys.

The trucks were huge tractor-trailer units, 18-wheelers, and a convoy might stretch for four or five miles.

The convoys I rode with weren't carrying conventional bombs.

They were moving a unique ordnance, and *lots* of it.

Packed into 12-foot long me
boxes and covered by tarps
the nature of this ordnance
was *unknown* to most of u

MP jeep escorts would drive in front, behind, and ranging alongside the trucks.

There was also a jeep carrying EOD personnel.

*EOD = Explosive Ordnance Disposal.

e never actually saw hat was inside the boxes.

We just knew the contents were *extremely* volatile.

KCHUNK

If jostled too much...

EEEEEEEEEEEEEE

RRRRT

EEEEEEEEEEEEEEEEEEEEEE

FLIK

VROOOM

EEEEEE

EODs would work frantically to re-stabilize the contents of the box...

EEEEEEEEEEEEEEEEEEEEEEEEEEEEEEEEEEEEE

...and disengage the alarm.

It was a nerve-jangling experience for everyone, and while MPs weren't privy to many details...

EEEEEEEEEEEEEEEEEEEEEEEEEEEEEE

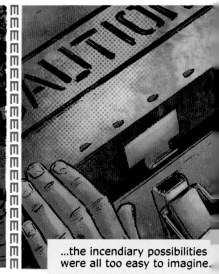

...the incendiary possibilities were all too easy to imagine.

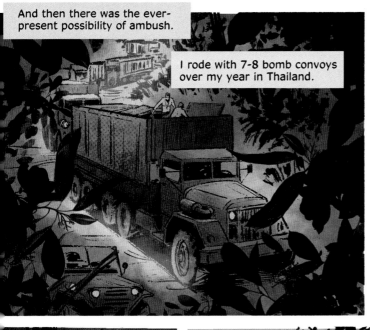

And then there was the ever-present possibility of ambush.

I rode with 7-8 bomb convoys over my year in Thailand.

But this is the one I'll never forget.

Our destination was Korat AFB, an all-day trip from the coast.

KLUNK

It was around midday, and we were starting to get into the mountains.

Here's the thing:

VROOOOOM

The convoys drove screamingly fast.

And they stopped for *nothing*.

KICK

AWOOO AWOOO

The mountain terrain on our run to Korat was always the scariest.

The roads were so steep that the trucks would drive nose to tail, pushing each other up steep grades.

VRRRRM

I remember how much I *hated* this part.

I didn't want to look down off the edge of the cliff...

VROOOM

tik

skkt

...so I looked *up* instead.

That's when I saw him.

I remember clenching in frozen anticipation of the bullet hitting me.

That alternate ending was not my destiny.

I did several more bomb convoy runs and finished my tour in late October of 1968.

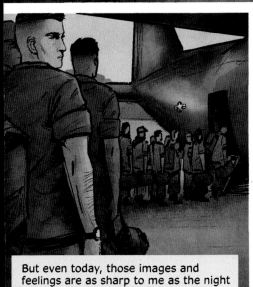

But even today, those images and feelings are as sharp to me as the night I dreamed them, over 50 years ago.

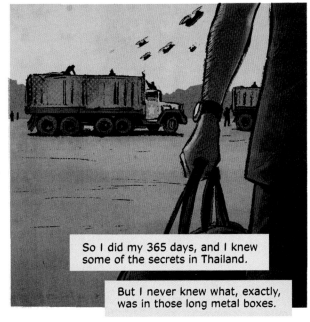

So I did my 365 days, and I knew some of the secrets in Thailand.

But I never knew what, exactly, was in those long metal boxes.

May 2010.

We touched down at **Bagram Airfield** sometime after midnight at the beginning of my rotation home.

My first deployment was absolute hell, but it was over.

We were turfed out onto the tarmac and pointed in the direction of the terminal.

The short walk to it was exhausting, doubly so since I had been up since about 0500 the morning before.

If you've never carried **50lbs** in each hand and almost **100lbs** on your back...

...I don't recommend it.

I saw guys from units with bases between Bagram and **FOB Bostick**, where I had just come from.

Hey, Lieutenant!

The only guy I knew was **Rodriguez**, from my platoon of infantrymen.

The young airman manning the terminal told us that every office on base was *closed* at this hour.

So unless we had someone from our unit coming to pick us up, we were out of luck as far as accommodations were concerned.

They answering?

What do *you* think?

Repeated phone calls to our unit's rear contingency on the other side of Bagram yielded no results.

Rod and I grabbed some space on baggage pallets and hunkered down for the night.

We'd slept in much *worse* places, after all.

I slept fitfully because they never turned out the lights.

Also because of the *nightmares*.

They were the product of a twisted coupling of trauma and the anti-malarial drugs that we were required to take, despite the suspected mental health side effects.*

The *meds* were the Army's fault, but the *trauma* was...

*In 2013, the FDA acknowledged that the medication can cause anxiety, depression, nightmares, hallucinations, and paranoia, and that these side effects can persist or even be permanent. Good looking out, Army.

...well, okay, the trauma was *also* pretty much the Army's fault.

It had been a *hell* of a year for my unit.

It may not sound like much to lose *eleven soldiers* from a whole cavalry squadron, but it is.

Most of the casualties in Afghanistan were, and still are, civilians, Afghan security forces, and *AAF*.

AAF (Anti-Afghan Fighters) was an acronym some staff weenie thought up as a catch-all for the dozen groups waging insurgent warfare against the US-installed Afghan government.

honestly, I don't recall really being sure who I was fighting from day to day.

Maybe someone in the *intel shop* could keep track.

But whether it was *Taliban* or *Hezb-e Islami Gulbuddin* or *Hezb-e Islami Khalis* or just a pissed-off local with an AK-47 and an axe to grind was largely immaterial when they were shooting at me. And shoot they did.

Two months into our rotation, we lost a sergeant first class on his fourth deployment. He had three kids and a pregnant wife at home.

It hit us like a slap in the face: if he could get killed, *anyone* could.

Our second KIA, though, was *devastating* to me.

A fellow platoon leader and good friend of mine was out on a routine patrol.

AAF shot and killed him.

...sir?

Remote outposts often have a refrigerated shipping container that the unit uses to keep food in.

It also acts as a makeshift morgue.

I sat with my friend's body in that container, staring at the black bag and trying to wrap my mind around the fact that he was right next to the meals I would be eating in a few days.

It wasn't enough.

I held the hand of a young man dying in our medics' meager aid station, his abdomen bleeding from half a dozen bullet wounds.

I *lied* to him that everything was going to be *fine*, because the docs had him now.

The medevac helicopter couldn't get to us for 12 hours due to the high volume of *enemy fire*.

I was amazed he lived long enough to get on it.

In the end, though, I was still a liar.

He died on the table in the operating room as a surgeon pumped his heart for him by hand.

We killed around *150 enemy fighters* that day.

We lost *eight soldiers* of our own and abandoned that outpost a week earlier than planned.

Putting those numbers side by side, you might get the impression that we *won*.

I *assure* you, dear reader, that we did not feel as though we won *anything*.

It should come as no surprise that I woke up in the rotary-wing personnel terminal at Bagram cynical, angry and cocksure.

I was also *starving*.

Rod and I were getting ready to head to the chow hall, with all its delicious big-base options, when--

AWOOOOOO

You have *got* to be shitting me.

INCOMING! INCOMING! SHELTER IN PLACE!

We were in the *most secure* place in Afghanistan.

HA HA

≷snerk≷

There would be no hundreds of enemy fighters overrunning Bagram Airfield.

In a nod to the fact we were still in a *war zone*, we put on our body armor and helmets, and slung our rifles.

What do *you two* think you're doing?

Going to *breakfast*.

Yeah.

We're *hungry*.

Look, the chow hall is **locked down** until they sound the **all-clear**.

You're **welcome** to walk the half-mile to **find out** for yourself, but...

Well, ☠⑥⚡#.

The logic was **unassailable**, even to grunts like us who could assail nearly any logic thrown at them.

The senior douchebag assured us that these never last more than an hour and that the dining facility would still serve breakfast when that hour was up.

We could wait an hour.

srumble

Hell, we could wait for **days**.

I personally had lived for **three days** on a **single MRE** after the enemy destroyed our food supplies when they overran our outpost.

Speaking of which...

...Two hours later, someone brought us a crate of MREs.

Beef ravioli: breakfast of **champions**.

While we ate, we tried again to call our unit reps at Bagram.

No dice.

So a **one-mile walk** it was, carrying our bags the whole way.

The three soldiers who **should** have picked us up hours before seemed **astonished** to see us.

But they checked us in and put us on a bus...

...to the other side of the base, where we claimed a couple bunks in a large clamshell tent converted to house *transient service members*.

I looked at the snoring, farting, sweating mass of humanity I found myself in.

It might not have been *home*, but it was familiar enough to offer a *strange comfort*.

My unit's area of operations during this tour was out on the hairy edge so the Army gave all sorts of *non-standard gear* to test:

Uniforms in an experimental camouflage pattern.

Smaller, lighter body armor.

Civilian hiking boots for patrolling in the Afghan mountains.

I changed into a standard Army uniform and boots and stashed my *combat swag* under my bunk.

An hour and a half later...

🐌⊘⚡# it!

Still, it was *hot* and we weren't stoked about an hour of walking.

So when we saw a pickup approaching...

At Bagram, there were a million *sergeants major* walking around with nothing better to do than yell at people for wearing *boots* that weren't *authorized*.

Meanwhile, Rod got some solid dope about a bus that came out here every 30 minutes and would take us the four miles to civilization.

Hey, Rod, chamber a *round*.

I got an *idea*.

KROOOM

SCREEE

Y'all need a *ride?*

Yeah, we're headin' to the *main post* but the *bus* don't seem to be *runnin'.* *

The truck had *aircon*.

And the Armed Forces Network radio DJ announced that *Ronnie James Dio* had died.

The truck dropped us at the main post and Rod and I walked to the Morale, Welfare, and Recreation tent.*

Thanks

There was something I had to do.

I checked my Facebook and fired off a message to the wife, then hit my brother up.

He was an officer in the Marine Corps, a pilot and a captain, and was posted here at Bagram.

He, along with our sister, was from my mom's first marriage and was about eight years older than me. I never really knew him growing up.

When my sister found out I'd be on the same base as him on my way home, she pointed out that Mom would murder *both* of us if we didn't at least *try* to get together.

he Morale tent has televisions and video game consoles, a small library of books, and rows of computers soldiers can use surf the web and chat with loved ones.

And then, there he was.

I recognized his *face* from *photos,* though I hadn't seen him in the flesh in *years.*

He saw me coming, my *gravel-gray* uniform sticking out in this land of *desert-tan* fatigues.

When he waved at me, I stuck out my hand.

It felt wrong immediately.

I should have gone for the *hug*, right?

What, exactly, is the *protocol* for greeting someone you barely know but share a mother with?

How have you *been?*

Good, you?

Good, good...

The pleasantries felt awkward and forced.

It's *great* to *see* you.

Yeah, *really* great.

Still, it wasn't the *worst* interaction I'd had with another human that day, thank you Air Force Security.

Uh, should we...?

The Marines' chow hall was smaller than the main one on Bagram, but seemed provisioned well enough.

The *barbecued chicken* was about as *appetizing* as any other military meal I'd had recently.

And the act of eating kept the conversation at what felt like a *manageable* pace.

And we *did* talk.

I knew he was a *pilot* in the Marines, but not the *type* of aircraft he flew, or *where*, or on what *kinds* of missions.

Turns out, he had flown in support of operations in *my area*.

Maybe even for one or two of the *patrols* I was on, without me ever knowing.

Oh, wait, do you *remember* when that was?

Lemme see...

I felt myself loosening up.

Maybe he *wasn't* some douchebag, after all.

Maybe he was just a guy like *me*, trying to do his *best* in a shitty war that, even back then, I knew was *unwinnable*.

He'd heard a little about my deployment. My *unit* was pretty *famous*, or maybe infamous. *Nobody'd* been in the *shit* that year like we had.

He *asked* me about it. To my *surprise*, I found myself *opening up*.

Telling him about getting *rocketed* and *mortared* and *shot at* almost every day.

About never being able to step *outside* without looking at the *mountains*, which always surrounded you...

Wow.

...scanning every shadow for a man lurking with a sniper rifle or a machinegun or a rocket launcher. About being terrified for your guys and yourself, but being brave because of them, too.

It all *poured* out of me, and as it did, I felt as though I were getting *lighter*.

Like I was putting down a ton of *rocks* I hadn't realized I'd been *carrying*.

At the end of my long rant he just *looked* at me and *smiled* and said he was *glad* I was okay.

Still, I knew he didn't understand, not *really*. How *could* he?

He was a pilot in an *aviation unit*, who carried around a little *9mm pistol* instead of the *rifle* with four-power magnification *scope* I was toting.

He had *eight hours* of mandated crew rest *every day* and probably hadn't worn *body armor* since he got here.

here wasn't anything *wrong* ith that, of course.

Hey, you want some *apple pie?*

It's *not bad.*

Takes all kinds.

But *hearing* isn't *knowing*, and knowing isn't *understanding.*

The apple pie was *pretty great*, actually.

(Pie was a big-base luxury.)

You think the *Afghan government's* got a chance?

I dunno...

Somehow the *surrealism* of the situation had *passed* and I was nore *at ease* than I'd been all day.

Well...

And then, of course, it was *over.*

Hey, you *okay?*

Yeah, I'm fine.

Maybe he *did* know.

Maybe he did understand.

Hey, *this* is for *you.*

We're the *only* organization that's *ever* been granted permission to use the *Playboy* logo.

We don't use it *officially* anymore, but we keep some of these *patches* around to remind us of our *heritage*.

want ou to ave it.

CAN DO EASY

VMAQ - 2

This is cool as ☘⊚◼✕!

t *absolutely* was the raddest thing that had happened to me in a *long* time, and the *best* gift I'd been given in recent memory.

We should get a *photo* for *Mom*.

Most of us carried *cameras*, because you never knew what kind of *crazy shit* you were going to see in Afghanistan.

So we set the timers, and posed, a little awkward all over again.

My job was mainly to patrol the city around the base's perimeter. Sometimes I would be posted at the front gates or checkpoints...

Next!

...Patting down potential suicide bombers, hoping to live another day.

Working those "suicide gates" was like this sick lottery that you didn't want to win.

Okay, go on through.

But for every suicide bomber, for every enemy insurgent...

...There were a thousand friendly faces in Kirkuk.

One of those friendly faces belonged to a teenager named *Brahim*.

Brahim was one of a group of kids that would follow us around on patrol.

American magazine!

One piece of candy!

I'd always entertain Brahim. I loved him.

Do you know *50 Cent?*

Wait, *what?*

But some of the guys in my squad, not so much.

No, I *don't* know 50 Cent.

Park!

We were in a war zone where enemy combatants didn't wear uniforms.

Come on!

I gotta *go.*

In my heart, I knew these kids weren't terrorists.

They were just trying to make the best out of a bad situation, like I was.

Brahim worked on our base as a janitor.

But he was biding his time to become an interpreter for the US Army.

It pays **$250 a week**, Dylan!

So *much* money! And also--

If you worked a certain amount of years as a translator, you'd get a United States visa.

Translator jobs came up regularly. Not because Iraqis were quitting...

...Because they were getting **killed**.

Brahim--

The terror groups would *execute* anyone they suspected of working with the Americans. Sometimes they would kill your family or your friends too.

I know, Dylan.

But with that *money* I can feed my *whole* family.

And I'd be *doing something* to end this war.

As the deployment went on, I learned a lot of things about this kid.

About all the friends and family members he'd lost in the conflict.

About how he was the sole provider for his household...

His house only had electricity every other week because of the rolling blackouts...

...and piss-poor plumbing, so even basic hygiene was a struggle.

...

As a cog in the war machine that had destroyed this kid's home country...

...I felt partially responsible for that.

He pointed out an ancient citadel that was built 2,000 years before Jesus was born.

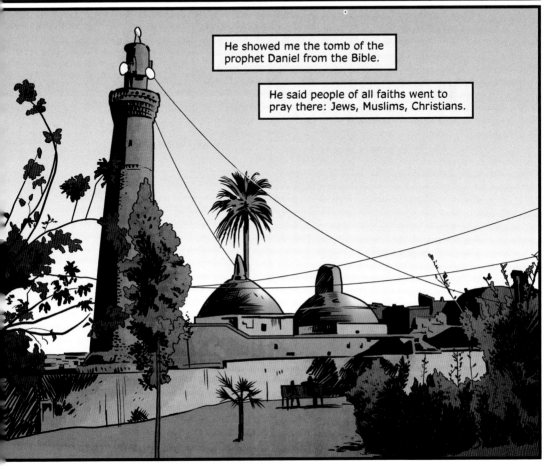

He showed me the tomb of the prophet Daniel from the Bible.

He said people of all faiths went to pray there: Jews, Muslims, Christians.

*Campbell, California.

We stopped for kabobs and fresh bread in a marketplace.

I don't know if I'm romanticizing this meal in my head, but to this day it's still the best meal I've ever eaten.

Towards the end of my deployment, Brahim finally got his wish.

He was hired as an interpreter.

Dylan! **Look!**

For me, that was bittersweet.

He was finally able to provide for his family.

But he had just volunteered for his own death.

Oh, Brahim. That's...

...Congratulations.

I knew I was leaving him to die.

I felt sick, but what could I do?

I wished him the best, got on a plane...

...and flew home.

For the next five years I struggled with my mental health.

I started abusing drugs and alcohol.

It was hard to keep a job because I was in and out of the court system.

There was even a period of homelessness.

But despite weekends in the county jail and different homeless shelters, I stayed a pretty decent student.

I was able to muscle my way through college.

Then one Saturday morning, I woke up to a dozen missed phone calls and text messages.

≡uugh≡

brrt brrt

...Mom?

What's up?

Obviously I didn't want to talk about my brother's murder, so I half lied.

I got out of the *military* a few years ago, and I got this *new job* in California.

Oh, *military?*

You go anywhere *special?*

Sure, I've been *all over* the world.

I most *recently* did a year in *Iraq.*

Iraq?

I'm from Iraq.

That's when I knew something was wrong.

Where in *Iraq* were you stationed?

In the *northeast*.

In this city called *Kirkuk*.

I'm from Kirkuk.

We sat there in silence, for miles.

I could *feel* him staring at me.

I kept thinking: did I harm one of his loved ones, intentionally or unintentionally?

Or maybe he was really anti-war. And if he was, could I blame him?

I was trying to avoid eye contact, so I looked out my window.

I saw us pass my exit.

Now I was *terrified*.

Hey, man. You *missed* the *exit*.

The driver didn't say anything.

He just took the next exit...

...drove a few blocks...

...and pulled over.

The red flags were going *off*.

It seemed like the driver was working up the guts to do something.

Whatever it was, I didn't want to be there to find out.

ROCKET PROPELLED
GRENADE NETTING

OSHKOSH (MRAP)
MINE RESISTANT
AMBUSH PROTECTED VEHICLE

IN THE END THIS PLANE WAS
FILLED WITH EQUIPMENT
AND PEOPLE AND SOLDIERS
ALL HEADING OUT OF
AFGHANISTAN

C17 - GLOBEMASTER
"MOOSE 86"

STAFF SERGEANT
JOSHUA BRONSON
HEADING HOME
AFTER HIS FOURTH
TOUR OF
AFGHANISTAN

Our Authors

Tyson Walsh is active Army, serving as an Operations Research and Systems Analysis Officer. He led a heavy armor platoon at Fort Carson, and commanded a light infantry company at Fort Polk. Now he seeks to combat veteran suicide through applied statistics and data science with The Objective Zero Foundation. Most of all, he has a wonderful wife and two high-energy children to keep him humble.

Robert Kent enlisted in the Air Force to avoid getting drafted into the Army. He served overseas from 1970-71 in Cam Ranh Bay, Vietnam. He now lives in Kissimmee, FL with his wife Debra. They have four children and six grandchildren.

Khai Krumbhaar joined the Army as an Arabic linguist just out of high school. After 27 collective months of deployment to Iraq and nearly 12 years of service (including a short stint with the Michigan National Guard) she was medically retired. She now splits her time between editing at The Geekiary, writing, and spending time with her partner and her service dog Fargo.

Ian Eishen enlisted in the Air Force in 2000 and is currently on active duty. He has served at locations all over the world, including the Philippines, Thailand, India, Germany, Ecuador, Iraq, Afghanistan, and Japan, and has spent much of his career testing and deploying emerging technologies to units across the Air Force.

Randy Brown is a 20-year Iowa Army National Guard veteran with one overseas deployment. His creative credits include his own poetry collection *Welcome to FOB Haiku: War Poems from Inside the Wire* and co-editing the recently released anthology *Why We Write: Craft Essays on Writing War*. As "Charlie Sherpa," he blogs about citizen-soldier life at www.redbullrising.com and about military-themed writing at www.aimingcircle.com.

Matthew Moores enlisted in the Marine Corps in 2009 and served with 2nd Tank Battalion until his medical retirement in 2016. He deployed with the 22nd MEU in 2011 and to Afghanistan in 2013. He is a full-time student, some-times writer, and prolific social media shitposter.

Benari Poulten is a comedian and Emmy-nominated writer/producer. Currently a Master Sergeant in the U.S. Army Reserve, Benari is a veteran of both Operations Enduring Freedom and Iraqi Freedom, having served on three separate deployments including to Iraq and Afghanistan. He is on twitter and instagram as @benarilee.

Juan Vaca is an American narrative designer specializing in interactive branching narrative for film, tv, and games. Juan advocates for authentic representation in all forms of storytelling. He also plays the jug, baritone, and nose whistle for The Rivertown Skifflers, "The Best Damn Jug Band in the Bay Area" (according to him).

Annie Blitzen is a long-time writer, first-time writer-who-actually-gets-something-published. She served in the U.S. Air Force from 2005-2009. She lives near Atlanta, GA with her wife (pictured herein) and child. She is a deeply ridiculous human person.

Jonathan Bratten is an engineer officer and National Guard historian from Maine. He enjoys hiking, writing, and forgetting that PowerPoint is a thing. He can be found on twitter doing very little at @jdbratten.

Brandon Davis Jennings is an Operation Iraqi Freedom Veteran from West Virginia. His other publications include *Operation Iraqi Freedom is My Fault*, *Battle Rattle*, and *Waiting for the Enemy*. He lives with his wife and daughters in Indiana and paints and writes when he's lucky enough to have time. Follow him on Instagram at @brandondjenningsart.

Jarrod Alberich is the creator of his own original comic book, *Hamilton vs. Burr: A Werewolf Tale*. Jarrod is also a trading card artist who has done work for Marvel & Upper Deck tradng cards. He earned the name "The Yard Sale Artist" from his propensity to paint and draw on yard sale-acquired items. You can find him podcasting on The Longbox Crusade Network as well as On Her Majesty's Secret Podcast.

Ray Patridge grew up in a rural area in southern Illinois. He was drafted at age 19 and spent a year at Fort Ord in California before being shipped overseas. After his service, he attended college and worked in the building trades. Since 1992, he has been raising sustainable grass-fed beef on his farm in Illinois. He is also a beekeeper. Life is sweet.

Stephen Cady is an active duty U.S. Army officer and bona fide nerd. Find him kicking around random parts of the world, putting fear into the hearts of evildoers.

Dylan Park is a writer/director hailing from the San Francisco Bay Area. Recent projects include contributions to the *New York Times* bestseller, *The Moth Presents: Occasional Magic* and writing for Paramount Network's *68 WHISKEY*. He's a graduate of Arizona State and attended the University of Southern California for graduate school. Dylan now resides in Santa Monica, CA.

Our Charities

The Air Force Assistance Fund provides support to the larger Air Force family in need (active duty, retirees, reservists, guard and dependents, including surviving spouses), in emergencies, with educational needs, or to help secure a retirement home for widows or widowers of Air Force members.

The Armed Services Arts Partnership aims to cultivate community and growth with veterans, servicemembers, military families and caregivers through offering free classes and workshops in a variety of arts, from drawing and writing through comedy and acting.

Paws & Effect is an Iowa- and North Carolina-based organization that raises, trains, and places service dogs with childen and veterans with disabilities.

The Objective Zero Foundation enhances social connectedness and access to wellness resources to combat suicide within the military community. Objective Zero is a mobile app that anonymously connects users to a nationwide network of peer support and wellness resources, tools and training.

The Special Operations Warrior Foundation ensures full post-secondary educational support to surviving children of special operations personnel and immdiate financial assistance to severely wounded special operations personnel.

The USO strengthens America's military servicemembers by keeping them connected to family, home and country, throughout their service to the nation.

All charities were chosen by our authors.

Incidental and chapter end drawings throughout, by Richard Johnson